Gareth Stevens
PUBLISHING

STORMS

# SNOWSTORMS

**by Jim Mezzanotte**

**Reading consultant:** Susan Nations, M.Ed., author/literacy coach/consultant in literacy development

**Science and curriculum consultant:** Debra Voege, M.A., science and math curriculum resource teacher

**Please visit our website, www.garethstevens.com.**
**For a free color catalog of all our high-quality books,**
**call toll free 1-800-542-2595 or fax 1-877-542-2596.**

**Library of Congress Cataloging-in-Publication Data**

Mezzanotte, Jim.
Snowstorms / by Jim Mezzanotte.
p. cm. — (Storms)
Includes bibliographical references and index.
ISBN-10: 0-8368-7914-7 ISBN-13: 978-0-8368-7914-8 (lib. bdg.)
ISBN-10: 0-8368-7921-X ISBN-13: 978-0-8368-7921-6 (softcover)
1. Blizzards—Juvenile literature. 2. Storms—Juvenile literature. I. Title.
QC926.37.M49 2007
551.55'5—dc22 2006033922

This edition first published in 2007 by
**Gareth Stevens Publishing**
111 East 14th Street, Suite 349
New York, NY 10003



Editorial direction: Mark Sachner
Editor: Barbara Kiely Miller
Art direction, cover and layout design: Tammy West
Photo research: Diane Laska-Swanke

Photo credits: Cover, title, pp. 5, 6, 9, 11, 14, 17, 18, 19, 21 © AP Images; p. 7 © Daryl Balfour/Photo Researchers, Inc.; pp. 8, 12 Scott M. Krall/© Weekly Reader Early Learning Library; p. 13 © Richard Walters/Visuals Unlimited; p. 15 © Weatherpix Stock Images



Printed in the United States of America

2 3 4 5 6 7 8 9 10 10 09 08 07

# Table of Contents



**Cover and title page:** A large snowstorm closes offices and schools in Canada. The storm's wind makes it hard for this person to cross the street.

# CHAPTER 1

## Here Comes Snow!

Have you ever seen a snowstorm? On a cold, winter day, gray clouds cover the sky. A few snowflakes begin to fall.

Soon many snowflakes are falling. You can hardly see through them. The snowflakes cover the ground, turning it white. A snowstorm has begun!

Snowstorms can be fun. If lots of snow falls, schools may close. After the storm, you can play outside. You can make a snowman or go sledding.

Snowstorms can be dangerous, too. Roads become slippery. People have car accidents. People cannot see well in a snowstorm. Sometimes, they get lost.

These children in New York City know the best thing to do when it snows. They go sledding in a nearby park.

Some snowstorms are very bad. These storms are called **blizzards**. During a blizzard, winds blow hard. Snow falls for three hours or more. Snow fills the air. We can only see things that are very close.

A bad snowstorm makes walking hard. One person uses an umbrella to block the wind and snow.

Snow falls in many parts of the world. It falls where the air is cold. Most snow falls in northern places during cold winters.

Snow can also fall in warm, southern places. In these places, snow falls on mountaintops. The air near the top of high mountains is cold enough for snow.

Snow covers the top of Mount Kilimanjaro in Africa. Giraffes live on the warm grasslands at the foot of the mountain.

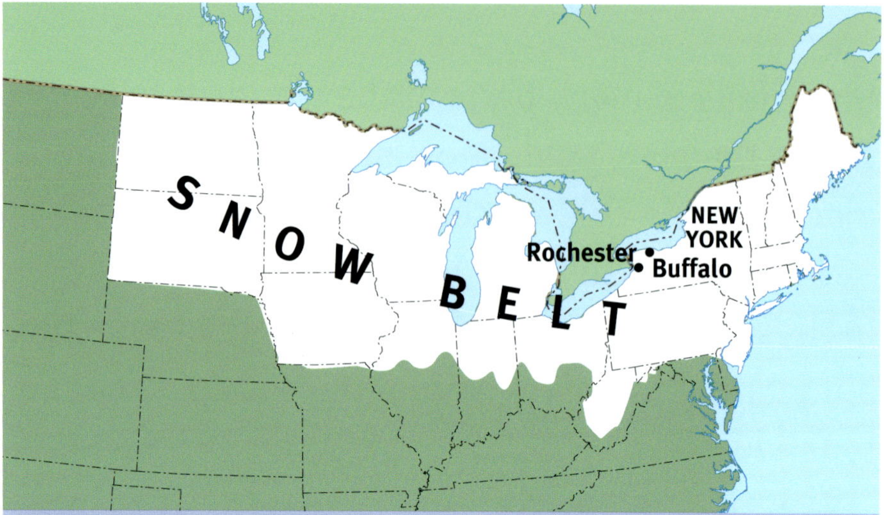


The areas in white on the map are part of the Snow Belt in the United States.

Snow has fallen all over the United States, but it hardly ever falls in southern states. Northern states get most of the snow.

Some northern states are in the Snow Belt. This area stretches from the Midwest to New England. States in the Snow Belt get lots of snow!

Two of the snowiest cities in the United States are Rochester and Buffalo, New York. In one winter, they can each get more than 10 feet (3 meters) of snow.

In 2001, Buffalo got about 7 feet (2 m) of snow in just five days! This man shovels piles of snow off of his house.

# CHAPTER 2

## Storms in Action

A snowstorm begins with clouds. They form when air rises from the ground. The air is warmer than air higher up.

The warm air is full of water. The water is not a liquid. It is a **gas** called water vapor. We cannot see water vapor.

The air cools as it rises higher in the sky. The water vapor turns back into a liquid. It becomes water drops.

If the air is very cold, the water drops freeze. They become tiny pieces of ice. These tiny pieces are called ice **crystals**.

High storm clouds float above Maryland. This storm will bring more than 6 inches (15 centimeters) of snow.

The ice crystals form clouds. The crystals join together, becoming snowflakes. The snowflakes fall from the clouds.

You might not see these snowflakes. Closer to the ground, the air may be too warm. The snow melts as it falls and becomes rain.

For snow to fall, the air must be cold. It must be near the freezing temperature of 32 °Fahrenheit (0 °Celsius).

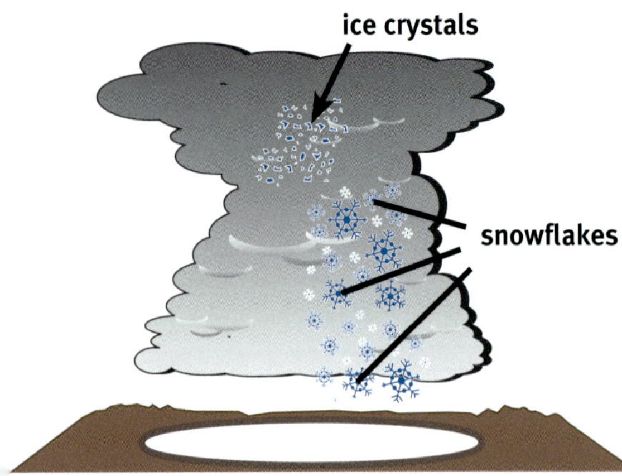


Rising water vapor condenses into water drops. The drops freeze and form ice crystals. Several crystals make up each snowflake.

Ice crystals join together in different ways. They make all kinds of snowflakes. No two snowflakes are the same. Each one is different.

Some snowflakes are big and fluffy. They look like stars. Others are small and hard. They look like tiny needles. All snowflakes have six sides.

The ice crystals in snowflakes look like pieces of glass.

Snowdrifts cover this street after a blizzard. People work together to dig out their cars.

When a blizzard hits, strong winds blow. They make a bad storm even worse! With no wind, snow falls straight down. But strong winds blow snow sideways. They blow snow already on the ground, too.

When winds blow, snow does not pile up evenly. In some places, the snow hardly covers the ground. In other places, the wind blows the snow into high piles called **snowdrifts**.

Sometimes, **sleet** or **freezing rain** falls instead of snow. The snow falls into warmer air and melts. It then falls through cold air. It freezes again, becoming sleet.

Snowflakes do not always freeze again. Sometimes, they fall as very cold raindrops. When this rain hits the cold ground, it freezes. It covers everything with ice.

Freezing rain leaves a beautiful coat of ice on trees. The heavy ice snaps off many of the branches, which crash to the ground.

# CHAPTER 3

## Bad Blizzards

Snowstorms cause many problems. People have trouble getting around. **Snowplows** try to keep roads clear, but the snow keeps falling. It covers the roads.

Cars and trucks sometimes slide around on snowy roads. They may get stuck or crash. Sometimes, drivers can see only the white of falling snow.

Airports may have to close. Snow covers the runways. Airplanes cannot take off or land. Schools and offices may close, too.

Heavy snow can damage buildings. It makes roofs cave in. Snow and ice can snap power lines and tree branches.

A heavy snowstorm knocked over these power poles near Buffalo. Workers have to go out in the cold to replace them.

Falling snow can hide the ice on roads. Cars on this snowy highway slide into each other and bring traffic to a stop.

During snowstorms, people may be hurt or killed. They might slip and fall. They may get in car accidents.

In some places, **avalanches** are a danger. A steep mountain has many layers of snow. A storm adds more snow. Suddenly, all the snow comes sliding down. The avalanche can bury people and buildings.

Strong winds can make the cold air feel even colder. People who are outside can become sick or die from the **windchill**.

When a snowstorm ends, the cleanup begins. Snow has to be cleared from roads. People have to shovel their driveways and sidewalks.

Power lines may have fallen down. Some people may be without power until workers fix the broken lines.

A snowplow works to clear a street in South Dakota. A blanket of snow covers the cars on the side of the street.

# CHAPTER 4

## Snow Safety

Scientists watch for snowstorms. An **anemometer** (an-uh-MOM-hu-tur) tells them how fast the wind is blowing. They use **radar** and **satellites** to track storm clouds. They try to decide when the snow will fall. Then they warn people that it is coming!

During a storm, scientists use a yardstick to measure how much snow has fallen. You can use one to measure the snow in your yard, too!

If a snowstorm is coming, people get ready. They buy extra food and other supplies in case they cannot leave their homes or they lose power.

When the storm starts, it will be cold and windy outside. The air will be thick with snow. The safest place to be is inside. You can stay warm while you watch the snow come down!

Snow fills these streets, keeping people inside. Many schools and offices close after a big snowstorm.

# Glossary

**anemometer** (an-uh-MOM-hu-tur) — a pole with cups that spin in the wind and measure its speed

**avalanches** — huge amounts of snow that come sliding down steep mountains or hills

**crystals** — solid pieces of a substance that have flat surfaces joined at sharp angles

**gas** — a form that something can take, such as water. Unlike a solid, a gas cannot hold its own shape. It keeps spreading out. Usually, a gas cannot be seen.

**radar** — a machine that shows where things are in a certain place

**satellites** — machines in space that send back pictures and information about places on Earth

**snowplows** — machines that clear snow away

**windchill** — the extra cold that a person feels when the wind blows

# For More Information

## Books

Blizzard. Wild Weather (series). Catherine Chambers (Heinemann)

Blizzards. Weather Update (series). Nathan Olson (Capstone Press)

Snow. Watching the Weather (series). Elizabeth Miles (Heinemann)

Whiteout! A Book About Blizzards. Amazing Science (series). Rick Thomas (Picture Window Books)

## Web Site

### Weather Wiz Kids: Winter Storms

www.weatherwizkids.com/winter_storms.htm

Facts, diagrams, and answers about storms. Weather games, experiments, and jokes, too.

**Publisher's note to educators and parents:** Our editors have carefully reviewed this Web site to ensure that it is suitable for children. Many Web sites change frequently, however, and we cannot guarantee that a site's future contents will continue to meet our high standards of quality and educational value. Be advised that children should be closely supervised whenever they access the Internet.

# Index



# About the Author

**Jim Mezzanotte** has written many books for children. He lives in Milwaukee, Wisconsin, with his wife and two sons. He has always been interested in the weather, especially big storms.